Southeast

CHEROKEES

By Marion Israel

Illustrated by Harry Timmins

Melmont Publishers, Inc.
Chicago, Illinois

Also by Marion Israel   about **The Tractor on the Farm**...

about **Sheep on the Ranch**

Apaches

Dakotas

Library of Congress Catalog Card Number 61-5013

"This Edition Printed ----1961"

TABLE OF CONTENTS
Pages

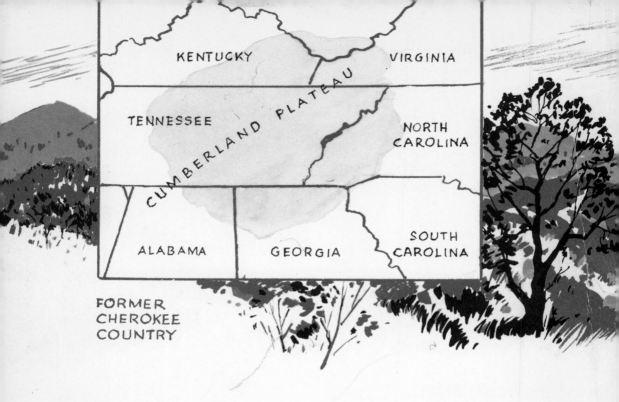

FORMER
CHEROKEE
COUNTRY

THE LAND AND THE PEOPLE

Before white men came to North America, the Cherokees lived in the valleys of the Blue Ridge Mountains. A few still live in a valley of the Blue Ridge. Most of them now live far away from their mountain home in the western state of Oklahoma.

Today Cherokees live like the white people around them. Some live on farms. Some live in towns. They have told us about the old ways. They have told us what Cherokees thought about their land, long ago.

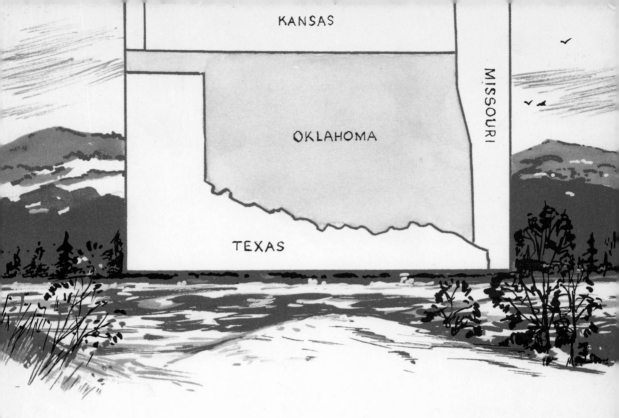

The great family that ruled the earth from the sky was good. Grandmother Sun warmed the earth, ripened the wild fruits, filled the day with light. Big Brother Moon pushed the dark away, lighted the night trail, kept people safe. Grandmother Fire warmed the house, cooked the meat and the mush.

Everywhere the Cherokees looked, there were mountains. Between the mountains were valleys, small and green. Rivers flowed through the valleys. Beside the rivers were towns.

THE TOWNS

There were seven towns with villages round about. In the center of the town was the town square. High above the square stood the council house. It stood on a built-up mound of earth. It had seven sides.

Each town had a town chief and seven town counsellors. In the council house, the chief sat across from the doorway. His counsellors sat on either side. Around the wall were seats for the people. On a small round altar of earth the sacred fire burned always.

The biggest town was the capital town. The town chief of the capital town was high chief of the tribe.

THE HOUSE

The houses of the town stood here and there outside the town square.

The father built the house. He built it of poles of hickory or cedar or pine. He plastered the walls, outside and in, with clay mixed with grass. He covered the roof with bark. He cut small square holes for windows and an opening for a doorway.

The fire burned in the middle of the floor. The smoke drifted out through a hole in the roof. Beds made of cane stood against the walls. Skins of bear and buffalo made the beds soft and warm.

The mother kept the house and cared for the children.

8

AROUND THE FIRE

PIPE

Life in one house was like life in all the houses. Every family lived in the ways of the tribe, given to the people long ago.

BASKETRY

Winter in Cherokee land was cold. The house was dark and warm and snug. At night the family sat on mats around the fire.

Perhaps the father chipped off some arrow points. Perhaps he carved the bowl for a soapstone pipe.

POTTERY

The mother wove a basket. While she worked, she told a story. The boy leaned against her soft, warm shoulder. Before she finished the story, he fell asleep.

ARROW POINTS

A JOURNEY IN APRIL

After the winter the earth woke up. The leaves and the grass came alive. In April, when the new moon first shone in the sky, the Cherokees held a feast.

From all the towns the people went to the capital town for the feast. The boy went with his parents and brother and sister.

The boy hoped they would go in the canoe, but the rivers were too swift. The family followed narrow trails above the flooding streams. Small piles of stones marked the trails. A daub of paint on a tree pointed the way.

In April the weather was cool. The father and the boys wore shirts and leggings and moccasins of buckskin. The mother and the girl wore skirts of deerskin and shawls of fur.

WORK IN SUMMER

After the feast the work of summer began. On some days the father went to the forest to cut dead trees for firewood. The boy liked to go with him. The father cut the wood, but he never carried it home. Carrying wood was the mother's work. It was her work, too, to bring water from the spring. The father never carried water.

Most of the time the mother was busy pounding corn. It took almost half a day to make enough corn meal for the day's bread.

THE PLANTING OF THE CORN

When it was time to plant corn, the town chief went up to the council house. The people hurried into the square to hear what he had to say. The chief named a day when the men of the town were to meet for the planting.

Then all the men were busy mending tools or making new ones. The father put a new handle on his stone spade. He twisted bark into a cord. With it he bound the spade to a hickory stick. He made a hoe from the shoulder bone of a buffalo.

The fields were beyond the town. No man's house stood beside his field. His house was in the town. No man called a field his own. The fields belonged to the tribe.

The town chief gave each family a field to hold for a year. A big family needed a big field. A small family needed a smaller field.

No man cleared and planted his own field. All the men together planted all the fields. An old man's field was planted for him. A sick man's field was planted for him. A widow's field was planted for her.

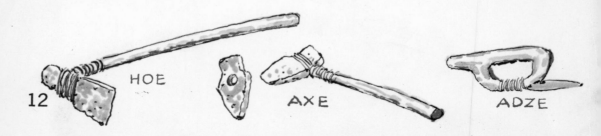

HOE   AXE   ADZE

12

PICK

KNIFE

HAFTING

CHIPPING
ARROW
HEAD

On the night before the planting the people danced to Old Woman of the Corn. A mortar stood in the town square. Men and women moved around it as if pouring corn or meal from a basket, held in one hand, into a bowl held in the other hand. The dance was a prayer for corn. Old Woman of the Corn understood.

On the morning after the dance the men met to plant the corn. They began work all together at one end of the fields. They dug the old weeds and burned them. They dug holes and dropped in the kernels of corn. They worked all day, every day, until all the fields were planted.

Old Woman of the Corn made the corn to grow. But the Cherokees helped.

Magicians prayed to the Woman of the East to send her rain down on the corn. They shook their turtle-shell rattles for the Thunder Men to hear. They laid swan feathers close to a stream for Big Brother Moon to see.

Every morning the town chief called from the mound for men to work in the fields. The men hoed the earth around the corn to keep it loose and soft.

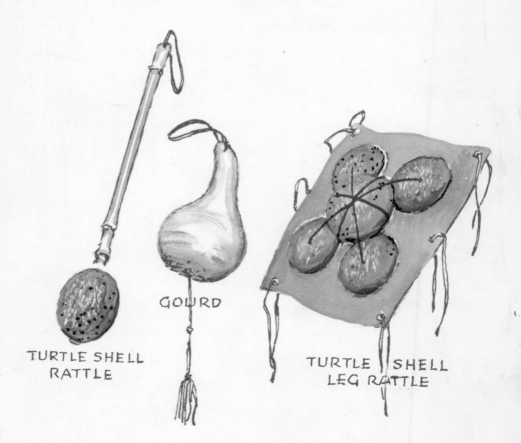

TURTLE SHELL RATTLE

GOURD

TURTLE SHELL LEG RATTLE

THE NEW GREEN CORN FEAST

In August the new ears of corn were sweet. But no one in town or village pulled an ear. New green corn must be eaten first by all the people together.

In the capital town the high chief and his counsellors made ready for the New Green Corn Feast.

The high chief sent seven hunters to the forest to get deer for the feast. One hunter wore a deer's-head mask. The hunters were in the forest six days.

The high chief sent messengers to the seven towns to call the people to the feast. The messengers brought back an ear of corn from each town. These seven were the first ears that were picked.

In August the rivers were quiet. The father made a new canoe for the journey to the capital town. The older boy helped him. They made the canoe of a log of pine or of poplar. They burned out the center of the log, then finished the hollowing with a stone adze. The bottom was flat. The ends were alike.

The family went to the capital town for the feast of the New Green Corn.

In August the weather was hot. The mother and the girl wore skirts and scarfs of mulberry bark. Here and there a bright feather was tied into the weaving.

The father and the boys wore deerskin breech-cloths and necklaces of shell beads. The father tied a new turkey feather in his scalp lock.

The mother packed the canoe with food and clothes. The father pushed it into the river. On the day before the feast the family landed at the capital town.

On the night before the feast the seven hunters brought in their deer. The messengers gave the high chief the first ears of corn from the seven towns. The high chief sat in the council with his counsellors. In the town square the people danced the New Green Corn Dance.

The next day a new fire was kindled on the altar in the council house. The chief placed on the new fire the seven first ears of corn. While they burned he gave thanks to Old Woman of the Corn.

Then all the people together ate deer meat and new green corn.

TRADERS

In summer Indians from other tribes came to trade with the Cherokees. Some carried salt, wrapped in buckskin, on their backs. Skin pouches hung from their belts.

The Cherokees brought out things they had made. Some brought meal to trade for salt. Some brought clay bowls. Some brought plates and spoons of wood. Some men offered pipes with carved bowls and long stems.

The trader sat on the ground in the town square. He spread a deerskin on the ground and opened his pouches on it. Here were shells from the ocean. Here were parrot feathers from a far-away land. Here were arrow points of black stone. Strange and beautiful things came out of the trader's pouch.

HUNTERS

In summer hunters went to the forest where the Animal People lived. The Cherokees thought that all the animals were people like themselves. But the Cherokees were the important people. They called themselves the Principal People.

The Cherokees hunted the Animal People. They hunted them with bows and arrows. They hunted them with blowguns. They kept the Animal People in fear of their lives.

The Cherokees ate the flesh of the Animal People and made clothes out of their skins. They made tools from their bones and their horns. The Cherokees hunted the Animal People, but they were afraid of them.

Before every hunt the hunter danced his prayer for a safe hunt and sang his magic song.

BOW AND
ARROW

BLOW-GUN

23

THE RIPE CORN FEAST

In September the corn was ripe. Each family gathered the crop from its own field. Each family gave some corn for the public storehouse. The rest was their own.

The storehouses in the town were full of corn. In every house there was corn for the winter.

From the capital town the high chief sent messengers to call the people to their thanksgiving feast. From all the towns the people came to the capital town for the feast.

In the capital town every family kept open house. Everyone who came to the door was welcome. The townspeople were busy getting ready for the feast. People from the other towns brought corn or beans or pumpkins. Some brought wild turkeys.

Seven hunters went to the forest for deer.

The town square looked like a little forest. A tall green tree stood in the center. It was made of green boughs tied to the top of a high pole. The high chief sat under a green arbor on a raised seat. His robe, leggings, and moccasins were of white deer skin. He wore a red cap on his head.

The feast lasted four days. On the first day the people marched, holding green boughs above their heads. On the other days the men danced magic dances for the good of the tribe. In the evenings, after the feasting, all the people danced in the square.

THE NEW FIRE

Summer ended with the Feast of the Great New Moon of Autumn. Winter began on the night the new moon first shone in October.

Soon after winter began, the high chief's messengers came through the towns. They told the people to make ready for the New Fire.

Then all the fires in all the towns were put out. The fires in the council houses were put out and the ashes swept away. Everything in the council houses was cleaned.

The fires in the houses had not once gone out all summer. Now the fires in all the houses were put out. The ashes were swept away. Every family cleaned the house and the household things.

From all the towns the people went to the capital town for the New Fire.

In the capital town the high chief sent seven hunters to the forest. He chose seven cleaners to clean the council house. He chose seven fire makers to make the new fire.

The fire makers scraped out a hollow in a block of wood. Into the hollow they dropped bits of old dry stalks of goldenrod.

A fire maker held a stick in the hollow and twirled it between his hands. One man after another twirled the stick. The wood grew hot. A spark gleamed in the goldenrod. The spark leaped into flame. The New Fire!

From the New Fire the fire makers kindled seven kinds of wood on the earthen altar. On the altar they burned wood from seven other kinds of trees. The high chief wafted the smoke to the east, to the west, to the north, and to the south.

After the festival the town chiefs took some of the new fire back to their council houses. The people took some of the new fire back to their own houses.

The mother laid wood on the floor of her house.
She kindled it with the New Fire. The family sat around
the fire. The house was dark and snug and warm. The
boy leaned against his mother's shoulder while she told
him the meaning of New Fire!

"After the summer the winter —
The new time.
All the houses are clean.
There is no uncleanness anywhere.
New Fire makes all hearts clean,
All people friends.
Quarrels are forgotten.
Hurts are forgiven.
Old fires of hate are put out.
There is no uncleanness anywhere."

For several years Marion Israel was engaged in the preparation of audio-visual materials for use in the schools of Los Angeles County, California. Her writing at that time consisted of supplementing pictorial and other materials with helpful background information for teachers. From this work grew the desire to prepare factual material of a similar nature for the children themselves.

In 1947 Miss Israel left the Office of the Los Angeles County Superintendent of Schools to devote herself to the writing of realistic non-fiction for younger children. She believes that real books for children, as for adults, must originate in the writer's feeling for the subject, and should communicate feeling as well as facts.

Marion Israel now lives in Northern California in a small foothill community on the edge of the Sierra Nevada Mountains. Here she delights in all wild creatures — birds, squirrels, foxes, deer. She abhors hunters. She is fond of wide open spaces, old prints, Chinese art; has not yet learned to like television.

Harry Timmins was sketching and drawing everything that came to hand even before he graduated from high school in Orleans, Nebraska. Upon graduation he accepted an apprenticeship in the art department of an engraving house in Kansas City. Succeeding moves took him to St. Louis, Chicago, New York, and Paris.

It was at the Chicago Art Institute that he received his formal art training. It was in Chicago, too, that he and a fellow artist founded the American Academy of Art, in which many of the best artists of the country have been trained.

In the 1930's Mr. Timmins entered the field of magazine illustration in New York. This work was interrupted five times by sojourns of from two to six months in Europe.

Mr. Timmins is the father of three grown children all of whom have stayed close to art. The daughter is married to an artist, the eldest son is an illustrator in New York City, and the youngest an art salesman and layout man in Los Angeles. Mr. Timmins now has a studio in Carmel, California, where he continues his work as an illustrator.